Prayer That Overcomes Obstacles
Practical Principles to Strengthen Your Prayer Life

Copyright © 2018 by Frank Ntare.
All rights reserved.

Published by:
Final Step Publishing LLC

PO Box 1441
Suffolk, VA 23439

For Worldwide Distribution
Printed in U.S.A.

ISBN: 978-0-9861250-9-6
Cover Design: LinaImaging Design

Prayer That Overcomes Obstacles

By
FRANK NTARE

Contacts
Revival Network International
P. O. Box 3112
Kigali, Rwanda,
East Africa.
Tel. (Mobile) +250 788 885 333
+250 786 167 002
E-mail: christworshipcentre@gmail.com

Dedication

To All Nations Awaiting the Awakening of Prayer Partners.

Acknowledgements

I would like to thank God the Father, the Son, and the Holy Spirit for making this piece of work possible. I also want to thank my dear wife Francoise for all the prayer and support during those tedious times of putting this together. Not forgetting my great friend Pr. Fred and his dear wife Ruth. May God bless you abundantly.

Table of Contents

Foreword I
Preface V
Chapter 1 – Introduction to prayer 1
Chapter 2 – Definition and Origin of Prayer 3
    The Victim Syndrome 3
    What then is Prayer? 4
Chapter 3 – Prayer Altars: The Abrahamic Strategy 7
Chapter 4 – Modern Day Revivalists and Revival Prayer Movements 13
    David Wilkerson 13
    W.J. Seymor 13
    Evan Roberts 14
Chapter 5 – Patterns of Prayer 17
    The Proper Pattern of Prayer 19
    Jesus' Pattern of Prayer 21
    Different Kinds of Prayer 24
    The Nature of Gods Answer to Prayer 25
Chapter 6 – Intercessory Prayer 27
Chapter 7 – Developing a Quiet Devotional Time with the Lord 41
    Spiritual Warfare 61
Chapter 8 – Covenant Positioning for Effective Prayer 63
    Examples of Covenant Terms and Conditions 63

Adam 63
Abraham 64
Appendix – All the Prayers of the Bible .... A

Foreword

I remember as a teenager finally getting the chance to wander out in our city alone. Until I turned 16 years of age I had always been under my parents' supervision. The truth is, even at 16 I would still be under their supervision, but I had more freedom. I had received my driving license, saved up for a used car, and now the whole world was open for exploration. Or at least I thought that I was going to be released to journey out into exploration. On my way to the car my father tossed me a phone. It was a small flip cell phone. I asked him, "Dad, what's this for?" He answered, "So you can call me if you need anything and I can reach you if I need anything." I took that phone, sat in the car and drove off into the wind. I would later gather with family and friends filling that time with exciting talk and lots of fun. I would attend classes where teachers would educate me on the ways of our society. I competed in sports while listening to coaches yell instructions from the bench. These were all great conversations however, in all of those cases I kept that cell phone with me. I knew that although I was engaged in these other conversations with friends, teachers, and coaches there was still no conversation more meaningful than the one I could have with my father. That cell phone was my connection.

In the same way that I was given a cell phone by my father, our Father God has given us prayer. Prayer keeps us connected so that we can call when we need Him or He can reach us when He needs us. It is a conversation that we have access to and is more comforting than the most dear family or friends. Psalm 18:24 says, "...there is a friend who sticks closer than a brother." Prayer provides wisdom beyond what any teacher could share. According to Proverbs 2:6 we know that the "...the Lord gives wisdom; from his mouth come knowledge and understanding." As much as I love competing in sports I have found that prayer is much more rewarding than any physical gain I could have. Paul once said in 1 Timothy 4:8 "For physical training is of some value, but Godliness has value for all things, holding promise for both the present life and the life to come." Essentially I have found that like a cell phone, prayer keeps us connected to God at all times.

It is this constant connection that has me so excited about introducing to you this book of prayer by Pastor Frank Ntare. I met Frank at an All Nations Conference featuring more than 30 Pastors from over 14 countries hosted in Franklin, VA. There I found him to not only be a great preacher but a man of prayer. He reminded me so much of the main character in Mark Batterson's book, "The Circle Maker." Batterson tells a story of a Jewish hero who was famous for praying for rain. During a first century B.C. drought that threatened to destroy his generation, Honi the circle maker drew a circle in the sand with his staff, dropped to his knees and offered this prayer:

"Sovereign Lord, I swear before your great name that I will not leave this circle until you have mercy upon your children."

Honi was criticized by many other leaders who felt his prayer was too bold, but it's tough to argue with miraculous results. As his prayer invaded heaven, rain descended to the earth. He did not accept the slack rain that came first or the flood like rain that came next. Instead he stayed in the circle until the steady and peaceful rain that he desired came. Honi is an example of what intentional and focused prayer can do. Never underestimate the power of an intentional prayer. Prayer can propel you over obstacles.

Honi reminds me so much of Pastor Frank. He has drawn a circle too. His circle is larger than his own home, and spans further than his own nation. He has drawn an international circle in which he now petitions God to bless us all. His prayer is for more than water rain, but for God to reign. He travels from place to place as God has instructs him to teach and demonstrate obstacle destroying prayers. Join him on this whimsical journey of prayer. You can trust his advice because it is not just theory it is what he practices himself.

This journey will take us through what prayer can do, how to engage in effective prayer and the exploration of various prayer types. Why go any further in this book you are wondering? Well, prayer is not only a communication device for him, it has many essential qualities for us all. After engaging in this conversation with Frank about prayer you too will be empowered to draw your own circles. You will draw circles around your family, finances, health, ministry, governments, nations and even the utter most parts of the world. Continue reading and you find that there are no obstacles that prayer won't launch you over. Christian philosopher and scientist Blaise Pascal (1623-62) wrote, "The heart has its reasons of which reason knows nothing ..." Here you will find that prayer has its reasons and you should not face another obstacle without having this foundational teaching on prayer that overcomes obstacles.

Dr Dwight Shawrod Riddick, II
Pastor First Baptist Church
Franklin, VA USA

PREFACE

Prayer Changes things! While this may sound like typical Christian rhetoric or Jesus jargon it is absolutely true. The world we live in often under estimates this powerful tool that God has granted us access to through Jesus Christ. While we may not use it as often or effectively as we ought to, I believe with the correct teachings we can reinstall the value of prayer into our world. Prayer is our ability to put God's word into practice for our everyday lives. Jesus understood the power of God's Word. So did David. And Moses. And the apostle Paul. And the prophets of the Old Testament. And countless other heroes of the faith. That's why they quoted Scripture in their private interactions with God. God never promised that life would be easy. He simply gave us access to prayer so that we could make it through hard times. Lao Tzu said it best," A journey of a thousand miles starts with a single step." Our first step to overcoming any obstacle must be prayer. Adversity is inevitable, but difficulties or misfortunes don't have to keep you from achieving your intended God ordained goals and finding the joy that Jesus promised in abundant life.

It's never about the size of the obstacle it's always about how you overcome these obstacles that makes all the difference.

Every challenge we successfully conquer serves to strengthen our will, faith and confidence;

and therefore our ability to confront future obstacles with faith.

So, the next time you find yourself standing in front of a huge mountain that feels impossible to climb--whether it involves your job, relationship, ministry or business-- refer to these principles on prayer tucked within the pages of this book to help you find your way and remember why you started on this journey in the first place.

Here are three things you'll discover as overall truths throughout the reading summarized for your convenience.

Praying God's Word solidifies your relationship with the Lord. In order to incorporate Scripture effectively into your prayer life, you have to spend time in its pages. You have to study God's interaction with people in good times and in bad. You have to examine the way he makes all things work according to his purposes. You have to come face to face with the fact that no situation is ever beyond his control. You have to make note of his goodness, his mercy and his grace. And you can't do those things without developing a deeper appreciation and love for the One who loves you beyond all measure and has a unique plan laid out for your life.

Praying God's Word fosters a healthy perspective toward Scripture. Hebrews 4:12 says "the word of God is alive and active." It's not some relic from a bygone era or an ancient religious history book. It's a tool, a weapon—a source of power, encouragement and inspiration that's every bit as potent today as it was three thousand years ago. To use God's Word in prayer is to tap into its power —

- to claim the promises that Moses clung to;

- to marvel at the wonders of creation that blew David's mind;

- to connect with the Creator and Sustainer of the universe as Job did;

- to find comfort and strength in our heavenly Father's presence as Jesus did.

Praying God's Word encourages an active and creative approach to prayer. Incorporating Scripture into your prayers shows that you're not content to rattle off rote words of praise, thanksgiving or supplication. Praying God's Word requires forethought and preparation. When you pull Scripture into your prayer time, you're saying to God, "This isn't something I want to rush through. This is something I want to savor, enjoy and make the most of." This is something that I want to encourage others to use in overcoming obstacles. This is why I believe that you must use prayer to overcome obstacles.

Chapter 1 – Introduction to Prayer

I believe God has birthed in me vision for the Revival Network International (RNI). It is committed to holding Schools of Prayer and prayer conferences around the world. We believe that like the disciples, we all need to learn how to pray. Many of us pray and many of us associate with praying people. It is important for us to know personally the reasons why we pray, what prayer is, and how to pray. Learning these important principles will help us to pray with understanding, depth, and consistency thereby producing results.

At the RNI School of Prayer, believers- new and seasoned believers alike- will learn; the many facets of prayer, the importance of prayer in the life of the believer as well as practical aspects of entering the Presence of God and bringing your request before Him.

Every believer is called to commune with God but not every believer knows how. In the RNI School of Prayer, we endeavor to teach the principles that will bridge the gap.

Luke 11:1 "One day Jesus was praying in a certain place. When He had finished, one of His disciples said to Him, 'LORD; teach us to pray...'"

Chapter 1 – Introduction to Prayer

Jesus' disciples urged their master to teach them how to pray. John had already taught his disciples the concept of prayer. How much more of us in this generation also go through similar schools of prayer? In fact, there is more need for prayer today than ever before because we are living in the end times, days of prophetic fulfillment. Jesus prophesied that in the last days there will be an increase of wickedness. This must be countered by an increase of effective fervent prayer.

Matthew 24:12-13 "Because of the increase of wickedness, the love of most will grow cold, but he who endures up to the end will be saved."

The battle of light against darkness, health against sickness, blessings against curses, righteousness against wickedness, success against failure, favor against rejection and life against death, has reached a level at which we cannot afford to do without effectual prayer.

Revelation 12: 7-12 "And there was war in heaven………… But woe to the earth and the sea because the devil has gone down to you! He is filled with fury because he knows that his time is short."

Now is time to engage the atomic power of prayer to smash the devil and level every mountain. Pray or Perish!!!

CHAPTER 2 – DEFINITION AND ORIGIN OF PRAYER

The Victim Syndrome

A clear illustration of the victim syndrome is the example of HIV/AIDS. The Human Immune Virus (HIV) is a stubborn virus. It resists every counter-force and causes an Acquired Immune Deficiency Syndrome (AIDS). But there are many virgins' world over who are living with this stubborn virus and the syndrome it creates. They have never been with a man/woman, they have never messed up their lives, but they are born by infected parents. They were born into an already messed up situation. They did not plan it, they do not like it, but they are living with it. It is awful and stubborn. It is a **victim syndrome**.

Genesis 4:26 "Seth also had a son and named him Enosh. At that time men began to call on the of the Lord.

Biblical records trace the origin of prayer as having begun during the days of Seth. He was born into a messed-up environment. His father and mother had fallen from the perfect set up that God had intended for humanity. They had been banished from the Garden of Eden, which literally means, 'A place of delight in God's presence.' Sickness, lack, poverty, conflict, sin, oppression, and every manner of things to worry about found their way into human circles. Seth was a victim of a situation he did not author. This is the **victim syndrome**. If nothing is done about the victim syndrome, then you remain a victim forever. Seth was determined to break free from the victim syndrome, but it was stubborn, and God's power and anointing was not accessible. Adam and Eve had created a gap between humanity and God. In his passion to break free, Seth discovers the concept of prayer; crying unto the name of the Lord for Him come and intervene in human affairs once again. It is Him who can do exceedingly, abundantly all we ask. (Ephesians 3:20). By this he was re-inviting the presence of the Lord. He was restoring fellowship that had been lost by those that came before him. No wonder, the great men of the bible came from the linage of Seth.

What then is Prayer?

Prayer is a medium through which man communes with God. Prayer is a dialogue, not a monologue. So, when we speak to God in prayer, we expect Him to speak back to us. God's feedback to us is more important than what we tell him.

Prayer is a legal invitation to God from mankind to intervene in human affairs. He demands partnership with man since, He delegated global authority to mankind. Every person operating under delegated authority must be in constant communion with the one who delegated him.

Prayer That Overcomes Obstacles

Psalm 115:16 *"The highest heavens belong to the LORD, but the earth he has given to mankind." Genesis 1:26-28 Then God said, "Let us make man in our image, in our likeness, and let them rule over the fish of the sea and the birds of the air, over the livestock, over all the earth, over all the creatures that move along the ground. So, God created man in His own image, in the image of God He created him; male and female he created them. God blessed them and said to them, 'Be fruitful and increase in number; fill the earth and subdue it. Rule over fish of the sea and the birds of the air and over every living creature that moves on the ground.'"*

Prayer is also designed for spiritual warfare.

Ephesians 6:10-18 "Finally my Brethren, be strong in the Lord and the power of His might. Put the whole armor of God that you may be able to stand against the wiles of the Devil. For we wrestle not against flesh and blood but against principalities, against powers, against the rulers of the darkness of this world, against spiritual wickedness in high places. Wherefore take unto you the whole armor of God that you may be able to withstand in the evil day and having done all to stand. Stand therefore, having your loins girt about with Truth and having on the breastplate of Righteousness and your feet shod with the Gospel of Peace. Above all, taking the shield of Faith wherewith you shall be able to quench all the fiery darts of the wicked. And take the Helmet of Salvation and the Sword of the Spirit, which is the Word of God. Praying always with all prayer and supplication in the Spirit and watching

Chapter 2 – Definition and Origin of Prayer

thereunto with all perseverance and supplication for all saints."

Prayer is designed for fellowship

2 Corinthians 13:14 "May the grace of the Lord Jesus Christ, and the love of God, and the fellowship of the Holy Spirit be with you all."

Three virtues in this text are attributed to the Godhead: grace, love, and fellowship. When man fellowships with God, there is an impartation of divine character, wisdom, anointing, and revelation.

Prayer of faith does the impossible. It accomplishes great exploits: prayer moves mountains and calm storms. Jesus taught His disciples that if they heard faith then nothing would be impossible for them. Then immediately after, He tells them that there is a stubborn situation that will not go away expect by prayer.

Mark 9:28-29 "After Jesus had gone indoors, His disciples asked Him privately, "Why couldn't we drive it out?" He replied, "this kind can come out only by prayer."

Your victories are just as many as your prayers

CHAPTER 3 – PRAYER ALTARS: THE ABRAHAMIC STRATEGY

In the Old Testament, the concept of altars can be traced in every generation. Even the wicked had demonic altars unto their gods. At the altar, the people of God gave sacrifices, they called unto the name of the Lord, they worshipped, they made covenants, they sought refuge, they sought counsel, mention it. The altar was a central part of their daily lives. Whatever was done at the Old Testament altar is still symbolic in the New Testament era. The altar is a place where:

The physical meets and interacts with the spiritual. In this interaction man receives from God strength, counsel, revelation, instruction, and any other kind of communication.

Genesis 12:7-8 "The Lord appeared to Abram and said, 'to your offspring I'll give this land.' So, he built an altar there to the Lord who had appeared to him……………there he built an altar and called on the name of the Lord."

Man enters covenant relationship comes along with covenant terms and conditions to be observed. It also comes along with covenant promises.

Chapter 3 – Prayer Altars: The Abrahamic Strategy

Genesis 15:18 "On that day the Lord made a covenant with Abram."

Man, accesses God's presence and fellowship through worship

Genesis 8:20 "Then Noah built an altar to the Lord and……… he sacrificed burnt offerings on it."

Man seeks refuge

1 Kings 1:50 "But Adonijah, in fear of Solomon, went and took hold of the horns of the altar."

These and many other scriptures underline the importance of the altar. In the New Testament setting, all this is symbolized by the Prayer altar. At this altar of prayer, man fellowships, worships, offers himself as a living sacrifice to God in prayer and intercession and we do all that was done on the Old Testament altar.

The prayer altar is a must in your personal life, your family, and your church. Spiritual leader and teacher Ngozi Nwoke speaks of various forms of the prayer alter in this way.

"Prayer is a must if you are to live a victorious life. God is calling people to build prayer altars in their lives. God is looking for a man who will stand in the gap that evil will not befall men. An understanding of what to expect when you rightly build a prayer altar will energize you to do so."

So I sought for a man among them who would make a wall, and stand in the gap before Me on behalf of the land, that I should not destroy it; but I found no one – Ezekiel 22:30 (NKJV)

But we will give ourselves continually to prayer and to the ministry of the word." – Acts 6:4 (NKJV).

Types of Prayer Altars

The altar of testimonies – Those who pray always will have testimony. Prayer is the processing plant for testimony.

The altar for speed accomplishment – Abraham's servant enjoyed divine speed after he prayed to God. Rebecca came out and did everything as the servant prayed (Genesis 24:12-27)

It is the altar of strength – Men of prayer are men of supernatural strength (Luke 22:40-43)

The altar of sanctification – The more you look at God in prayer, the more you look like Him. If you keep seeking the face of God in prayer, your desire for sin will disappear. In all probability, the more prayerful you are the more sanctified you become (Luke 9:28-29, Malachi 3:3)

The altar of possibilities – God is the God of possibilities. When you pray and stay on the altar you will see the glory and get the answers (Jeremiah 32:27, Mark 10:27, Mark 9:23)

Chapter 3 – Prayer Altars: The Abrahamic Strategy

The altar that alters things – It is the control room to press switches for change. Elijah prayed and there was no rain for three years. He prayed again and rain came (James 5:17-18)

The altar of visions and revelations – Men of prayers are men of visions and revelations. Where these don't exist, you have confusion and uncertainties (Proverbs 29:18, Habakkuk 2:1-2, Acts 10)

The altar of dominion – it is the winning altar; you have dominion over all, including dominion over sin. It is a set platform to take charge of your day and life in general. Jesus would pray in the night and in the morning have dominion over affairs of the day (Luke 5:15-16, Luke 6:12-13)

The altar of divine direction – Through prayer you obtain guidance and divine direction. Jesus was never trapped because He was always led and guided by God. It is wisdom to be led than to be delivered (Psalm 32:8, Isaiah 48:17)

It is the altar of grace – You obtain favour and mercy at the altar of prayer. Nehemiah prayed for mercy and favour before the King and God granted him. The king released him to go and rebuild the city of Judah (Hebrews 4:16, Nehemiah 1:4-11, Nehemiah 2:1-8)

The altar of revival – Every revival is birth and sustained at the altar of prayer. When God moves, everything moves (Joel 2:28-32, acts 4:24-31, Acts 5:12-16).

How long you stay in God's presence determines the results you get. The prayer altar enables you to dwell in the Lord's presence and enjoy the wonders of His presence. It is the express access to all that God can ever give to man. He shall call upon Me, and I will answer him; I will be with him in trouble; I will deliver him and honor him – Psalm 91:15 (NKJV) If you desire answers from God, then you have to call upon Him, and altar of prayer enables you to do so.

The altar of turnaround – In Acts 16:25-34, Paul and Silas prayed unto God and the prison doors were opened, the chains of the prisoners were all loosed. When the keeper of the prison saw the doors open, he wanted to kill himself and Paul restrained him and spoke the word of God to him and his family. This led to a big turnaround in the life of the man and family: they were saved. It is the altar of divine intervention – on mount Zion there is deliverance and holiness and the people of God possess their possessions (Obadiah 17). At the altar you come to a place of appointment with God for divine intervention, to possess what belongs to you in Christ.

The altar of divine favor – When you cry out to God in prayers for His kingdom sake, He ensures that what other people are running after instead of Him come to you in abundance (Matthew 6:33). God will cause you to find favor before God and man.

The altar of empowerment – Signs and wonders are by-products of spiritual empowerment, which is a direct product of prayers. After Jesus fasted and

Chapter 3 – Prayer Altars: The Abrahamic Strategy

prayed for forty days in the wilderness, He returned in the power of the Spirit and news of Him spread about the whole region (Luke 4:14). He did great and mighty things because He has been empowered at the altar of prayer.

Altar of prayer is a meeting point between God and man, where God is ready to communicate with you as a father would with his son. It is a place where you can get anything the word of God says has been freely given to you by reason of redemption by the blood of Jesus. The altar is a place where you are empowered to flow in the supernatural. Heaven must first hear you before signs and wonders can be wrought by you. So, make the altar of prayer your number one daily schedule, and please don't be in a hurry to leave.

Chapter 4 – Modern Day Revivalists and Revival Prayer Movements

David Wilkerson

David Wilkerson of New York spent too much time watching T.V through he was still longing for God to use him. So, one-day God came around and told him about his T.V addiction. Apart from his quiet time in the morning, Jesus said he would need to spend two hours hitherto spent in the evenings to God and God's anointing came upon his life and he was launched into New York as a mighty evangelist to the ghettos. So, he converted T.V time to prayer time and God's power came upon him.

W.J. Seymor

W.J. Seymor, the black man whom God used to bring back the Holy Ghost. Revival at the turn of this century had initially gathered cartoons together for his pulpit in the early days of his ministry. One day, he told God he wanted to see a mighty revival in his land. God told him to double the time spent in his quiet time from one hour to two hours. At the end of two months, God told him to add another hour. He prayed three hours per day for about three months then God told him to double the three hours to make six hours of daily prayer for revival. After months of

Chapter 4 – Modern Day Revivalists and Revival Prayer Movements

traveling in this protracted, the spirit and the Pentecostal power descended on him and through his extraordinary ministry, an awesome sweeping revival broke out in America. He was the one God used to bring restoration of the gift of tongues to the church of Christ early this century.

Evan Roberts

Evan Roberts a 26-year-old college student in preparation for the ministry he was baptized with a passion for souls and the spirit of prayer. His parents and friends could not understand him. He kept much to himself alone with God. He said, "something drew me irresistibly to the condition of the lost world." This same "thing" drove him into such passionate intercessory prayers that rent the heavens and poured out revival flames that engulfed the whole nation of Wales in a few months. It was reported that within the first five weeks of the revival, between 20,000 to 30,000 souls were saved. Across Wales talented actors and actress failed to draw sizable attendances. In one town, the entire football team was disbanded because its members were converted and were more concerned for their souls. Soccer matches, and other shows were cancelled or rescheduled because everyone was going to church. Dance halls and night clubs in various places were deserted. In some districts, magistrates had no cases in court. Crime rates fell drastically. The horses and mules working in the coal mines had to be restrained because they were not used to the kindness now being manifested by the formerly wicked drivers. Evan Roberts was the instrument God used to ignite revival flames that spread like wild fire across the whole nation. Satan was soundly defeated in the whole land. Why? Because someone yielded himself to the spirit of prayer, and the Holy Spirit could arrest, conquer and subdue a young man on his knees. Oh Lord, what about several young people wasting away today? No holy fire on their souls, not eternity conscious, out of step with God, in deep romance with the world and spending their youthful lives and opportunities on things that will not stand the test of eternal wisdom. Listen to Evan Roberts on how the revival erupted. "Do you see that rug?" Pointing to a rug with a deep hole in it, there began the Welsh revival. I wore that hole on my knees as I prayed for the visitation of the Holy Spirit in convicting power upon the people. For five months before the revival began, I prayed agonizingly for the Holy Spirit. Each day, I spent 3-6 hours in prayer. I woke up each night at 1 a.m. and prayed until 4 a.m., sometimes until 9 a.m. Call this <u>GRACE</u> but do not forget to call it <u>PRICE</u>. Without a readiness to pay the price, one may obtain such grace in vain. (2 Corinthians 6:1 "As God's fellow workers we urge you not to receive God's grace in vain.")

Chapter 4 – Modern Day Revivalists and Revival Prayer Movements

Chapter 5 – Patterns of Prayer

It has been well said that the church cannot go forward unless it is on its knees. When we properly understand that we can accomplish nothing for the kingdom of God unless it by the Holy Spirit working through us, then we also then understand the absolute necessity of prayer. Martyn Lloyd-Jones said that prayer is "beyond any question the highest activity of the human soul."

The Sermon on the Mount looks at the Proper Purpose & Practice of Prayer. In Matthew 6:5,6 we found that Jesus instructed us not to follow the example of the hypocrites whose hearts were far from God but sought to give the appearance of being pious by putting on a show of their prayers. The Proper Purpose of Prayer is to speak to your heavenly Father and seek His approval. Prayer is about talking with God and not about impressing men.

In verses 7,8 we found that the Proper Practice of Prayer begins with a proper understanding of God and His love for us. We can go to Him with confidence that He knows our needs before we even pray, and therefore as we pray according to His will He hears us and will answer us. This is in contrast to both the Gentiles who repeated their prayers over and over again trying to get God's attention and the Pharisees who gave long prayers trying to impress God.

Chapter 5 – Patterns of Prayer

We do not impress God by either the length or eloquence of our prayers. What God wants is modeled for us by Jesus in verses 9-13. These verses are often referred to as the "Lord's Prayer," however, it is not "His" prayer but a model of prayer given to teach his disciples how to pray. That is what Jesus been doing throughout this passage. In 6:5 Jesus says, "When you pray." In 6:6 He says, "But you, when you pray." In 6:7 He instructs them, "when you are praying," and in 6:8 He tells them, " before you ask Him."

Here in Matthew 6:9 Jesus again addresses His disciples in the command voice saying, "Pray, then, in this way." He was requiring them to pray according to the model He was giving them. So then, this is not really "the Lord's Prayer," but rather "Jesus' Pattern of Prayer." Why spend the time to make this point? Because some believe that the prayer itself has power because Jesus prayed it. It is this kind of thinking that leads to the same meaningless repetition that Jesus spoke against back in verse 7. This prayer has no power because Jesus prayed it. First, Jesus did not pray it. Jesus had no need to ask for forgiveness. He gave it to His disciples as a pattern for their prayers. Second, we need to be very clear that there is no power in the words themselves of this prayer or any prayer. The power is always in God, not in the words. I hope you understand this is directly contradictory to what those in the Positive Confession movement will tell you. The teachings of such people as Larry Lea, Paul Yongi Cho, Robert Schuller, Kenneth Copeland, Kenneth Hagin, Charles Capps, Robert Tilton, Paul

Crouch, etc, etc, etc, are absolutely wrong on this. Words in and of themselves neither contain spiritual power nor do they carry or transmit spiritual power. Words are simply a means of communication. The spiritual power is always in God. Romans 8 even tells us that when words fail us the Holy Spirit intercedes with the Father for us. Prayer is not an incantation of magical formulas.

So this is not a prayer for us to repeat but to use as pattern just as Jesus says in His introduction to it – "Pray, then, in this way," or as it is translated in the KJV, "After this manner therefore pray ye." We are to pray after the manner of this prayer. We are not to repetitiously repeat its exact words.

The Proper Pattern of Prayer

"Our Father Who art in heaven, Hallowed be Thy name. Thy Kingdom come. Thy will be done, On Earth as it is in heaven. Give us this day our daily bread. And forgive us our debts, as we also forgive our debtors. And do not lead us into temptation, but deliver us from evil. (For Thine is the kingdom, and the power, and the glory, forever. Amen)."

This simple prayer of less than 60 words in Greek (67 in English) covers all of what prayer is about. First, it tells us what we need to know about our relationship with the One we are praying too including what His position is and what He is like. Second, it tells us the subjects that are part of prayer by telling us what is important in life, what we have

Chapter 5 – Patterns of Prayer

need of and the source of that need being met. Third, it covers all aspects of time – past, present and future.

It is a prayer gives as a pattern, but it is not the last time Jesus would teach about the patterns of prayer.

JESUS' PATTERN OF PRAYER

Jesus is our model in prayer just as He is our model in every aspect of the Christian life. If it was necessary for Jesus, the Son of God, to pray regularly how much more is it necessary for us to pray regularly? Jesus' disciples urged their master to teach them how to pray. John had already taught his disciples the concept of prayer. How much more must we of this generation also go through similar schools of prayer?

Luke 11:1 "One day Jesus was praying in a certain place. When He had finished, one of His disciples said to Him, 'Lord; teach us to pray....'"

Jesus, the greatest teacher of all time, taught them a pattern of prayer:

Matthew 6:9 "This, then, is how you should pray:
"Our Father in heaven,
Hallowed be your name,
Your kingdom come,
Your will be done on earth as it is in heaven.

This is the first major part in Jesus' patter of prayer. It is surprising to note that in this first part you and I do not feature anywhere. So, could it be that we are not considered at all in Jesus' pattern of prayer? No, look at the second major part; it is about us.

Matthew 6:11-13 "Give us today our daily bread.

Chapter 5 – Patterns of Prayer

Forgive us our debts, as we also have forgiven our debtors.
And lead us not into temptation,
But deliver us from the evil one.

This part is entirely ours. It caters for every area of our lives. God is so concerned about us, but first, we must ensure:

That His name is glorified in our thoughts, in our own words and deeds. We must keenly observe our attitude towards God and His word. If we have the right attitude, we shall make the right decisions which will in turn influence our actions.

That God is supreme ruler of our lives. There is no kingdom without a king. For His kingdom to come, God must assume first place in whatever you do.

That His will is done as He intends it, not as you want it.

If these conditions are not fulfilled, then we lose the legal right to petition Him to:

Give us
Forgive us
Lead us
And deliver us

After it is all done, all the honor and glory go back to God. Consider the ten lepers who were healed by Jesus. Only one of them came back to give

Prayer That Overcomes Obstacles

the glory back to Him. When he did so, Jesus made him whole (Luke 17:11-19).

Verses 15-19 "one of them, when he saw he was healed, came back, praising God in a loud voice. He threw himself at Jesus' feet and thanked him – and he was a Samaritan. Jesus asked, "Were not all ten cleansed? Where are the other nine? Was no one found to return and give praise to God except this foreigner? Then He said to him, "Rise and go, your faith has made you well."

Chapter 5 – Patterns of Prayer

DIFFERENT KINDS OF PRAYER

The Holy Spirit revealed, through the Apostle Paul, that there is not just one kind of prayer but many kinds.

Ephesians 6:18 "And pray in the spirit on all occasions with all kinds of prayers and request. Be alert and always keep on praying for all saints."

Just as a soldier carries several weapons in times of war, so we also need to be ready to practice various kinds of prayer in each situation. Here are some of the various kinds of prayer:

Prayer of Devotion
Payer of Petition
Payer of Supplication
Prayer of Intercession
Prayer of thanksgiving
Prayer of praise
Prophetic prayer
Prophetic intercession
Corporate prayer
Spiritual warfare prayer
Prayer of deliverance

THE NATURE OF GODS ANSWER TO PRAYER

God answers all prayers in five categories. God hears our prayers, but He answer in diverse ways:

The Direct Answer (1 Chronicles 4:9)
The Delayed Answer (Genesis 15:2-5)
The Denied Answer (1 Samuel 16:1)
The Different Answer (Matthew 26:39)
The More Than Enough Answer (1 Kings 3:7-14)

Chapter 5 – Patterns of Prayer

CHAPTER 6 – INTERCESSORY PRAYER

Type of Prayer Intercessors Do:

Now it is up to the individual intercessor to decide what type of prayer they are going to be doing in their times of intercession with God. It could be one type of prayer or several different types of prayer all weaving in and out of the prayer time. The following are just a few of the ways intercessors carry out the prayer work of God.

First and foremost Intercessors stand in the gap between man and God and pray on man's behalf. They seek always to reconcile, people, places, events, nations, etc with God and His plans and purposes. Now they do this standing in the gap in different ways and please note that the following is not a comprehensive list.

Intercessors prayerfully agree here on earth with the plans of God. This means that when God shows them what He is or rather what He wants to, they pray in agreement with His will. Remember that Jesus left His authority upon the earth with the church. He also left us with the ministry of reconciliation. God is always looking to reconcile people, situations, events, countries etc. So because we are the ministers of reconciliation and we are the ones who carry Christ's authority, He often will

Chapter 6 – Intercessory Prayer

reveal what he wants to do to the intercessor so that the intercessor can AGREE with God and open the way for the reconciliation of whatever kind to come forth. Remember Ezekiel 22:30

And I sought a man among them who should build up the wall and stand in the gap before Me for the land, that I should not destroy it, but I found none.

God wanted someone to agree with him to NOT destroy the land but he found no one. SO agreeing with God for his plans and purposes to come forth is one type of prayer intercessors do.

Intercessors can decree out the will plans and purposes of God. This is where they verbally speak forth God's purposes. Often this will go hand in hand with some type of prophetic act that brings release of the work of God.

Prophetic acts are a type of intercession that is really like prayers acted out in the natural. They are usually associated with what God is doing in the heavens and can range from things like stomping your feet upon the ground because the Lord is stamping out evil in a certain region to blowing kazoos to help clear out an open heaven.

Another type of Intercessory Prayer is repentance and standing in identification repentance on behalf of those they are interceding for. This is often done by intercessors during their prayer time.

Travailing is also a type of prayer work done by intercessors. This is more like a birthing type of prayer where the intercessor is actually praying in BODY and Spirit and there are manifestations in their body that correspond with what God is doing in the heavens. This is a major type of breakthrough intercession.

If you have never travailed before it is rather hard to describe what it is like and exactly what is going – it is similar to burden bearing but it is different in that it usually brings breakthrough and doesn't last as long. It can include weeping, moaning, shaking, sobbing, actually a whole host of manifestations. It is praying strongly in the spirit and it affects our physical bodies beyond the reasoning of our minds.

Some intercessors that go through travail don't always know the immediate reason for it but the reason is often revealed after the travailing time of intercession has ended.

Fasting is also a way intercessors will do the work of the Lord be it fasting from food or sleep-that time is devoted to prayer on their assignments and following the Lord.

Some Intercessors who have high level of authority and large sphere of influence do engage in spiritual warfare praying at the leading of the Lord and they do work with angels in that warfare.

Central to EVERY Intercessor is Worship because worship is the highest form of warfare that an intercessor can do and is central to most of their activities. So agreeing, decreeing, prophetic acts, travailing, warfare all of these are just a few ways that intercessors pray during their times with the Lord.

God is looking for people who will make themselves available and just say "YES" to taking time to pray for His desires. Maybe YOU are just the person He is looking for!

Administrative Intercessors:

The administrative intercessors have the gifts of leadership, giving, exhortation, faith, and administration. They serve as the *spinal cord* in the Body carrying orders to other members. They coordinate and form prayer chains, telephone networks, newsletters and crises lines so everyone will be notified and encouraged to pray. Without these administrators, much of the intercession we experience today would lack the order and follow through these steadfast men and women of God provide.

Cafeteria-Style Intercession:

These are men and women who intercede cafeteria style. Their prayer lives are continually changing Like chameleons, they do not conform to any particular mode or method. They are pliable and flexible in the hand of God. They can discern the Spirit's direction, whether in travail, warfare or prayer lists. These intercessors easily enter the flow of the Spirit. Even new believers can intercede effectively in this way.

Crisis Intercession:

These intercessors pray for emergencies and can recognize when traumatic events have occurred. Like an E.M.S. ambulance driver, this emergency intercessor is always on call. Emergency intercessors sense the urgency in every crisis. They are the search and rescue team for those who are wounded on the spiritual battlefield. Their gifts might include: prophecy, mercy, faith, healing, pastor, service. We must have these intense people who receive emergency calls and send immediate intercessory help.

Geographical Intercessor:

Today, God is calling more intercessors for the nations than has ever been recorded by the church. These are the evangelists in the Body of Christ. They may have a gift mix of evangelism, prophecy, faith and mercy. These intercessors stand in the gap for different nations of the world to pray in the last great revival before Christ's return.

Mercy-Motivated Intercessors:

From a merciful heart mercy-motivated intercessors find great satisfaction praying for any event, city, nation or situation needing the mercy of the Lord. They breathe compassion and empathy into the spiritual lives of others and are able to touch the heartache of another with encouragement and love. Mercy-motivated intercessors often move in the gifts of counseling, healing, giving and helps

Prayer-Evangelism Intercessors:

These intercessors pray toward evangelism, ministry and service to others. They act as the 'knees' of the Body. They can cross the street or the city on their knees with prayer for the lost. Their prayers often result in sending workers to the right people in the right place for the right reason-bringing others to Christ. Their gifts often include faith, service and evangelism.

Prayer-List Intercessors

Some intercessors pray through prayer lists. They tend to have the gift of administration or teacher or teacher mentioned in Romans 12. These prayer-list intercessors tend to be disciplined as they faithfully pray through the assignments God gives them on their ordered prayer lists. Occasionally they will get emergency requests and prophetic instruction, but their priority is to be persevering for the people, places and issues on their prayer lists.

Prophetic Intercessors

There are 'prophetic intercessors' who seem to hear from God almost as much as they speak to God. Exhortation, faith, wisdom, words of knowledge and discernment flow from the prophetic intercessor. Paul mentioned the eyes and the ears of the Body in 1 Corinthians 12. He points out that if the whole Body were an eye, there would be no hearing. With those who are the eyes and ears (prophetic intercessors), God often shares the secrets of His heart and the strategies of His work. God reveals His plans to them. At times He reveals the plans of the enemy, as well.

Special Assignment Intercessors:

(Assigned to an individual) have a special assignment to pray for leaders, such as religious, political or social leaders. They have a nurturing pastoral gift. They love to minister and shepherd in prayer, and quite often intercede with great compassion. The primary concern of the special assignment intercessor is the protection and care given the Body of Christ. They also feel deeply about the leaders for whom they pray. At times they become emotionally attached to them. Leadership can misunderstand them if they do not appreciate the shepherding heart of these prayer intercessors.

Chapter 6 – Intercessory Prayer

Warfare Intercessors:

Some intercessors are prayer warriors involved in spiritual warfare, which requires the revelatory gifts spoken of in 1 Corinthians 12. These gifts might include: faith, word of knowledge, discernment of spirits or prophecy. Prayer warriors are aware of the battle in the heavenlies (see Eph. 6:12). If the Body of Christ does not understand and learn from these intercessors, they will not see the spiritual battle developing. Like a spiritual radar installation, a prayer warrior is constantly surveying the heavenlies. When he or she locks in on prayer concern, this warrior has a gift to be an eye in the Body of Christ. The Lord reveals enemy targets that need to be demolished. Like the 'smart bombs' of Desert Storm, this kind of intercession is activated by the Spirit of God to hit a specific target.

1. **Issues Intercessors** — Standing against injustices. The 'issues' are what make you weep and pound the table!
2. **List Intercessors** — You find freedom in structure! As soon as you hear a prayer request, you're looking for a pen.
3. **Soul Intercessors** — God's Midwives - you love to pray for people to choose everlasting life.
4. **Personal Intercessors** — Spiritual Guardians - You are a personal intercessor who can be trusted with confidential information, in order to pray for another person.
5. **Financial Intercessors** — Faith for Finances/Funding - You've been anointed by God to summon funds on behalf of others.
6. **Mercy Intercessors** — The Heart people - you are God's living stethoscopes. You can hear/feel the pain of others and want to extend the mercy of God to the root of that pain.
7. **Crisis Intercessors** — Paramedics of Prayer - You rush in and out of the throne room with urgent requests on behalf of others - acting as watchman for God's people. You are the ones He can wake up in the middle of the night to pray for someone you may or may not even know!

Chapter 6 – Intercessory Prayer

8. **Warfare Intercessors** — The Military Might of the Kingdom - You fight to usher in truth by establishing God's authority in places where the enemy has a 'strong' hold on people, places or situations.

9. **Worship Intercessors** — Sacred Romancers - You access heaven's power, thru worship and bring hope to the hopeless. You silence the voice of the enemy and release the voice of the Beloved over people and situations.

10. **Government Intercessors** — Watchmen for Politics and the Church - You are the watchmen who prayerfully uphold the leaders in the church and political arenas where destinies are forged.

11. **People-Group and Israel Intercessors** — Prayer Shepherds for Ethnic Groups. God is calling intercessory shepherds to lead the way in prayer for entire people groups. You're heart leaps when you think of certain nations or ethnic groups and you find yourself praying for them to be touched by God as a nation or group.

12. **Prophetic Intercessors** — Trusted with the Secrets of God - You pray the things on God's heart; then, under His direction you report the words, thoughts, images and

actions He releases you to share - at His discretion.

Apostolic Intercessors – Those who call for the change of government in the House of God, in cities, regions and nations.Combines with Governmental, Breaker anointing and Warfare Intercessors.

Bridal Intercessors – Those who give expression to the Song of Solomon; e.g. Ana; Mary of Bethany.Praying for and keeping intimacy with the Lord as a priority in intercession.

Breaker Anointing Intercessors – Those who carry the breaker anointing in intercession. Particularly used in a forerunner/apostolic context to break open hardened regions so the 5 fold ministry of Ephesians 4:11can begin new works.

Church Revival Intercessors – Those who call for revival in the Body of Christ located in particular cities;e.g.the church in New York,the church in Miami, etc.

Crisis Intercessors – Those who have wisdom to know the prayers on God's heart in crisis times.

Financial Intercessors – Those who call for the transfer of wealth into the Kingdom.

Chapter 6 – Intercessory Prayer

Family Intercessors — Those who bring families and family issues before the Throne. Concerned for the integrity of the family and marriage in society.

Glory Intercessors — Those who call for the outpouring of glory in the last days with signs, wonders and miracles so that the glory of God will cover the earth.

Governmental Intercessors — Those who pray for governmental change. They must have a pure heart and proper motivation due to principalities they will encounter in the intercession. See Apostolic.

Issue Intercessors — Those who pray for such issues as repentance, abortion, racism, injustice, etc.

Judicial Intercessors — Call for justice for the poor, the unborn, the oppressed, etc. Overlaps with governmental and issue intercessors. Most of this has to do with bringing the government of God into the world. Can overlap with other areas since it's about the scales of justice being called forth.

List Intercessors — Those who pray for others' prayer requests in list form.

Leader Intercessors — Those who pray for leaders of nations, governments, etc.

Mercy Intercessors — Those who call for mercy for people and situations both personally and corporately.

Personal Intercessors — Those whom God gives a ministry leader or particular person to pray for over long periods of time.

People Group Intercessors — Those who pray for unreached people groups, cultures or nations worldwide e.g. the Dalit's of India, Amazon tribes, Generation X ers, etc. would be considered unreached people groups.

Prophetic Intercessors — Those who see and pray out of revelation the current burdens on God's heart; they receive both the revelation and identify it for the corporate body.

Research Intercessors — Those who are usually called to research historical situations and patterns before praying; e.g. broken treaties, war patterns, spiritual mapping, etc.

Restoration/Reconciliation/Salvation Intercessors — Those who pray for the restoration of all things in the lives of people, situation and nations as they are calling for reconciliation with God. Intercessors with a strong evangelistic mantle.

Chapter 6 – Intercessory Prayer

Warfare Intercessors – Those with an anointing for spiritual warfare to break through demonic realms in prayer. Spiritual warfare has time dimensions which are different from intercessions. Intercessions are carried over longer periods of time with warfare interspersed. These intercessors will come forth at key times in the intercessions.

Worship Intercessors – Those who are given to the place of worship as their intercession; e.g. Harp and Bowl type, those called with a Zadok anointing in intercession, etc

CHAPTER 7 – DEVELOPING A QUIET DEVOTIONAL TIME WITH THE LORD

In chapter two, we learnt that prayer is a dialogue and that when we speak to God in prayer, we should expect Him to speak back to us. This feedback from God is His response to our prayers and it is more important to us than what we have to say to Him, for He knows our needs even before we pray. That is why it is important to listen to God and hear what He has to say to us. Every listener must be silent at a time to hear properly. Sometimes God speaks in a gentle whisper; and we need to pay extra attention to hear Him. That is why every believer must develop a quiet devotional time with the Lord.

1 Kings 19:12 "…………After the fire came a gentle whisper"

Psalms 46:10 "Be still and know that I am God, I will be exalted among the nations, I will be exalted in the earth."

Habakkuk 2:20 "But the Lord is in His holy temple, let all the earth be silent before Him"

Psalms 37:7 "Be still before the Lord and wait patiently for Him… "

The bible says a gentle and quiet spirit is of great worth in God's sight.

Chapter 7 – Developing A Quiet Devotional Time with The Lord

"Instead it should be that of your inner self, the unfading beauty of a gentle and quiet spirit, which is of great worth in God's sight.

PRAYER AS COMMUNION

Prayer is more than communication with God. It is communion with Him. God created humankind in His image and likeness to have fellowship with Him. Prayer is the means to that communion. The Psalmist expressed it this way: "Deep calls to deep in the roar of your waterfalls; all your waves and breakers have swept over me." (Psalm 42:7) This is not an observation from nature but a description of fellowship with the Almighty. From the depths of His Spirit, God calls to the depths of our spirits and solicits a response. The result is deep, intimate fellowship with God through worshipful prayer.

Chapter 7 – Developing A Quiet Devotional Time with The Lord

PRAYER THAT WORSHIPS GOD

Prayer as communion is prayer that worships God. Just as the Psalmist used the imagery of waterfalls to describe the deep communion of man and his Maker, Jesus used the imagery of a wellspring within the heart of the believer to describe the way worship springs forth from the depths of one's being and connects with God. In talking to the Samaritan woman at the well, Jesus said that the water he could give to a person to quench his spiritual thirst "will become in him a spring of water welling up to eternal life." (John 4:13b) I believe He is referring to worship by which the believer connects with God, the source of eternal life. For a few verses later Jesus said to her, "God is spirit, and his worshipers must worship in spirit and in truth." (verse 24) It is our regenerated spirit quickened by the Holy Spirit that wells up in worship to our God and Savior. He said to those gathered in Jerusalem for the Feast of Tabernacles, "If anyone is thirsty, let him come to me and drink. Whoever believes in me, as the Scripture has said, streams of living water will flow from within him." (John 4:37b-38) For the sake of explanation, the next verse reads, "By this he meant the Spirit, whom those who believed in him were later to receive." (verse 39a)

When we move from prayer as communication to prayer as communion, we move from dialogue to intimacy. It is like moving from the living room to the bed chambers. Anyone who has experienced the Baptism in the Holy Spirit knows this experience firsthand. Anyone who has not but who thirsts for God is invited into this intimate communion of spirits.

Those who define prayer as "talking to God" would say that this teaching has digressed from discussing prayer to discussing worship. As we said earlier, though, prayer is not talking with God. Such dialogue is only one facet of prayer. We have defined prayer as "the passageway to a living and working relationship with God." Since worship connects our spirits with God, the source of life, worship is an aspect of prayer. In fact, worship is the spirit of prayer. The Lord's Prayer begins with the hallowing of God's name (see Matthew 6:9) and ends with a threefold doxology of worship ascribing to God the kingdom, power, and glory. (See verse 13b.)

Chapter 7 – Developing A Quiet Devotional Time with The Lord

PRAYER THAT SUBMITS TO GOD

Prayer as communion is prayer that submits to God. To have communion with someone is to share something in common with them. The prophet Amos raises the question, "Do two walk together unless they have agreed to do so?" (3:3) We cannot walk with God and commune with Him unless we agree with Him. And what is it that would stand in the way of such agreement? Isaiah writes: "But your iniquities have separated you from your God; your sins have hidden his face from you, so that he will not hear." (59:2) It is sin that hinders communion with God. So then, prayer as communion is prayer that submits to God through humility and repentance of sin. God's response to Solomon's Prayer of Dedication for the Temple appealed for the only kind of prayer that would restore broken communion between God and His people. He beckoned, "If my people, who are called by my name, will humble themselves and pray and seek my face and turn from their wicked ways, then will I hear from heaven and will forgive their sin and will heal their land." (2 Chronicles 7:14)

To submit to God goes beyond repentance of sin. It also includes deferring to God's will. This is a part of the prayer of submission that enables communion with God. The very heart of the Lord's Prayer petitions for the coming of God's kingdom and the establishment of His will. (See Matthew 6:10.) Not only did Jesus teach us to pray this way. He did the same in the Garden of Gethsemane when he prayed, "Not as I will, but as you will." (Matthew 26:39) It is only as we defer to the will of God that we can have communion with Him. So, in our prayer lives the worship of God must lead to submission to Him.

As with Jesus in the Garden of Gethsemane, the prayer of submission will frequently be a prayer of self-denial. Self-denial is always a part of communion with another person. We cannot be selfish and have fellowship with another. A relationship requires two people to work at denying self and deferring to the other. God expressed the ultimate in self-denial when He became a man in Christ and gave His life at Calvary to bridge the gap and reestablish communion with us. Now He calls for the same response from us. Will we deny ourselves, take our cross, and follow Him? (See Luke 9:23.) If it is God's rule that we want in our lives, then our prayer lives must be an exercise in self-denial.

Chapter 7 – Developing A Quiet Devotional Time with The Lord

PRAYER THAT RELATES TO GOD

Prayer as communion is prayer born out of our relationship with God. Our relationship with God through Christ is the key to answered prayer. In John 15, Jesus depicted himself as a life-giving vine and His followers as branches drawing their life from Him. Later in the same chapter, He called them friends and said that He had made known to them everything the Father had revealed to Him so that they could lead lives that would bear fruit for God's glory. And what is the result of this life of abiding and fruitfulness? "Then the Father will give you whatever you ask in my name." (verse 16b) When we have a relationship with God in which we are God's friends, receive revelation from him, and lead lives that bear fruit for His glory, Jesus says that the result will be a life of continuous answered prayer.

To maintain an unbroken relationship with God that is essential to a life of answered prayer, it is necessary that we maintain a right spirit toward others. Scripture is clear that if we don't love our Christian brother and sister, we don't truly love God. (See 1 John 4:20.) This being the case, God uses prayer as a means to mending strained or broken relationships. In the Lord's Prayer, we petition: "Forgive us our debts, as we also have forgiven our debtors." (Matthew 6:12) Here again is an exercise of self-denial in prayer. We must deny ourselves the "right" to have unforgiveness in our hearts against others if we are to maintain harmony in our relationship with God.

Our relationship with God through Christ is the basis for our confidence in prayer. The writer of Hebrews states that because of the atonement of Christ by which we are restored in our relationship with God, and because of Christ's faithful high priestly intercession for us, we are invited to "come boldly unto the throne of grace, that we may obtain mercy, and find grace to help in time of need." (Hebrews 4:16b)

This facet of prayer as communion with God has great attraction and great promise. God invites us into a life of prayer in which we experience intimate and ecstatic communion with Him, bow our hearts in submission to His will, live in harmony with Christian brothers and sisters, maintain a pure heart toward everyone, an embrace a life of continuous answered prayer. This is God's promise to us when He invites us to experience prayer as communion

Chapter 7 – Developing A Quiet Devotional Time with The Lord

PRAYER AS COOPERATION

A third facet of prayer invites us to join with God in the making of history. Prayer is cooperation with God. It is to position oneself to receive revelation of God's purposes and to release His will in the earth. As Walter Wink states, "History belongs to the intercessor."

This aspect of prayer harks back to what we said earlier about the prayer life of Jesus. His prayer life brought him into a working relationship with His Father. He received revelation from the Father concerning the words He was to speak in His teaching and the miraculous works He was to do in ministry. (See John 7:16; 14:10, 24; 10:32.) Once Jesus received revelation of God's purposes, all He needed to do was speak the word and the power of the Holy Spirit was released to accomplish the work. This is what He meant in saying, "The words I say to you are not just my own. Rather, it is the Father, living in me, who is doing his work." (John 14:10b)

To say that prayer is cooperation with God is to say that we, like Jesus, will hear words from the Father, see the works the Father is doing, and release them into the earth. And how does this take place in the lives of believers? It happens in conjunction with prayers of petition and prayers of intercession.

PRAYERS OF PETITION

To say that prayer is cooperation with God is to say that our prayers are a means that God uses to accomplish His will. One way that this happens is through prayers of petition. We ascertain just what it is that God's wants done, and we petition Him in prayer to do it.

In order to cooperate with God through prayers of petition, we must first receive revelation of what He wants to do. Such revelation becomes the foundation of effective petitionary prayer. This truth was communicated by Jesus to His disciples using the analogy of the keys of the kingdom.

After Jesus had spent considerable time with His disciples living with them, teaching them, training them, anointing them, and sending them out in ministry, He popped the all-important question one day.

"Who do people say the Son of Man is?" (See Matthew 16:13b.)

That was easy. It required no special revelation. They answered, "Some say John the Baptist; others say Elijah; and still others, Jeremiah or one of the prophets." (See verse 14.)

Chapter 7 – Developing A Quiet Devotional Time with The Lord

Now came the real question. "But what about you? . . . Who do you say I am?" (See verse 15.)

They were His disciples. He had poured Himself into them. Did they know who they were dealing with? One knew. Peter replied, "You are the Christ, the Son of the living God." (See verse 16.)

This wasn't what the people said of Jesus. How did Peter know? Jesus answered that question in His response. He said, "Blessed are you, Simon son of Jonah, for this was not revealed to you by man, but by my Father in heaven." (See verse 17.) Peter recognized Jesus' identity only because God revealed it to Peter.

What does all this have to do with prayer? Jesus next statement begins to make the application for us. He said to Peter, "I will give you the keys of the kingdom of heaven; whatever you bind on earth will be bound in heaven, and whatever you loose on earth will be loosed in heaven." (See verse 19.) Jesus made this same statement to all of his disciples two chapters later and then followed it with an encouragement to petitionary prayer. He said:

I tell you the truth, whatever you bind on earth will be bound in heaven, and whatever you loose on earth will be loosed in heaven. Again, I tell you that if two of you on earth agree about anything you ask for, it will be done for you by my Father in heaven. For where two or three come together in my name, there am I with them. (See Matthew 18:19-20.)

This exchange between Jesus and his disciples teaches us several things about effective petitionary prayer. Let me summarize them in bullet form:

- When we submit ourselves to God to become disciples of Jesus, we come to know by revelation from the Father just who Jesus is and what He is up to in the world.

- Such revelation of the identity of Jesus and of His work in the world entitles us to the keys of the kingdom by which we bind the works of the Enemy and loose the work of God in peoples' lives.

- This act of using the keys of the kingdom to bind Satan's works and loose God's work in people's lives takes place through prayers of petition offered in agreement with other believers gathered in Jesus name.

When we pray in the spirit of Jesus enlightened by an understanding of who He is and what He desires to do, we can have full confidence that our prayers will be answered. His promise is, "You may ask me for anything in my name, and I will do it." In this

Chapter 7 – Developing A Quiet Devotional Time with The Lord

way, petitionary prayer becomes a means by which we cooperate with God to accomplish His will.

PRAYERS OF INTERCESSION

Another way that we can cooperate with God through prayer is by prayers of intercession. An intercessor is one who "stands in the gap" between God and humankind. Ultimately, Jesus is the Intercessor between God and humankind as His atoning sacrifice has provided the way for sinful, fallen humanity to be reconciled to God. As the risen Lord, He is ascended to God's right hand where He acts as our High Priest continually interceding for us before God.

As followers of Jesus, we are called to be a "royal priesthood" (see 1 Peter 2:9), which means that we are to intercede for each other and for those who have not yet become followers of Jesus. We intercede for others through prayer that appeals to the atonement of Christ, stands upon the promises of God's Word, resists the Enemy's strategies to thwart God's will, and receives the grace of God for the meeting of the needs of those we are praying for.

The classic Old Testament text regarding intercession is from the book of Ezekiel. God wanted to spare His people from judgment for their idolatry and backsliding, so He sought for someone to intercede for them -- but, His seeking was in vain. The Lord said to Ezekiel:

I looked for a man among them who would build up the wall and stand before me in the gap on behalf of the land so I would not have to destroy it,

Chapter 7 – Developing A Quiet Devotional Time with The Lord

but I found none. So I will pour out my wrath on them and consume them with my fiery anger, bringing down on their own heads all they have done, declares the Sovereign LORD. (See 22:30-31.)

This passage clearly teaches that God wanted to spare His people but could not because He couldn't find someone to cooperate with Him. The cooperation He was looking for was described with two images:

1. He needed someone to "build the wall." That is, someone had to fortify the people spiritually so that they would not be vulnerable to the Enemy's temptations to idolatry and backsliding.

2. He needed someone to "stand . . . in the gap." That is, someone had to mediate between God and His backslidden people in order for them to be forgiven, restored, and reconciled to God.

We are to cooperate with God through prayers of intercession. It is in intercession for others that we "build the wall" and "stand in the gap." That is, our prayers result in believers being strengthened spiritually to resist temptations to idolatry and backsliding. We build the wall. Our prayers also result in the lost being reconciled to God. We stand in the gap. For Jesus atonement has made provision for both, and we intercede in His name.

PRAYER AS COMBAT

Thus far we have discussed aspects of prayer that focus upon God: we communicate with Him, commune with Him, and cooperate with Him. We come now to consider a facet of prayer that moves outward with God against the Enemy. Prayer is combat. Prayer is not only a means for establishing the reign of God in the earth but also of enforcing Satan's defeat.

Spiritual warfare is at the heart of the Lord's Prayer. Jesus taught His disciples to pray, "Your kingdom come, your will be done on earth as it is in heaven." (See Matthew 6:10.) In the Greek text of this verse, the verbs are are the forefront of their respective clauses. A literal reading would be "Come, your kingdom; Be done, your will . . . ." This sentence structure in New Testament Greek gives an imperative thrust to this petition of the Lord's Prayer. We are boldly declaring in prayer that God's kingdom will come and His will shall be done.

When it comes to prayer, we are to be among the spiritually forceful who rend the kingdom of God from the obstructing clutches of Satan who would try to hold back God's blessing and favor from us. Jesus said, "From the days of John the Baptist till now, the kingdom of heaven has been forcefully advancing, and forceful men lay hold of it." (See Matthew 11:12.) God does not withhold His kingdom from us. He freely gives it. Jesus' said, "Do not be afraid, little flock, for your Father has been pleased to give

Chapter 7 – Developing A Quiet Devotional Time with The Lord

you the kingdom." (See Luke 12:32.) It is Satan who tries to withhold God's kingdom from us, and prayer is the means by which we violently rend it from him.

Satan is a master deceiver. He disguises His schemes through craftily weaving them into the fabric of human culture so that they become the "way of the world" in which we live. We who believe in Christ are not of this world but have a heavenly citizenship. (See John 17:14 and Philippians 3:20.) Therefore, our prayers are to be a form of protest against the status quo that runs against the grain of God's will. In an article titled "Prayer: Rebelling Against the Status Quo," David Wells states:

What, then, is the nature of petitionary prayer? It is, in essence, rebellion against the world in its fallenness, the absolute and undying refusal to accept as normal what is pervasively abnormal. It is, in this its negative aspect, the refusal of every agenda, every scheme, every interpretation that is at odds with the norm as originally established by God.

Jesus emphasized the role of prayer as protest in His parable of the widow and the unjust judge. (See Luke 18:1-8.) The judge represented the status quo. He had neither a fear of God nor a love for people. He wasn't the slightest bit interested in upholding justice in the poor widow woman's behalf. But, she continued coming to him day in and day out protesting the injustice done against her and demanding, "Grant me justice against my adversary." (See verse 3.) Finally, the judge complied just to get her off his back. Jesus used this parable to teach an important lesson about prayer as protest. He asked, "Will not God bring about justice for his chosen ones, who cry out to him day and night? Will he keep putting them off? I tell you, he will see that they get justice, and quickly." (See verses 7 and 8.)

When it comes to dealing with an ungodly status quo, prayer is an effective means of protest. While social activism and public protests may change society for the better through blood, sweat, and tears, warfare prayer goes right to the root of the problem and disarms the spiritual forces that cause people to treat others unjustly. This is why Paul, in a classic text on spiritual warfare, lists among the four categories of demonic spirits that we wrestle with "the powers of this dark world" and "the spiritual forces of evil in the heavenly realms." (See Ephesians 6:12b.) For just as demonic spirits do battle in the heavenly realms in an attempt to prevent God's kingdom from coming to the earth (see Daniel 9-10), they also work in the earth to darken peoples' minds to the revelation of God ways. (See 2 Corinthians 4:4.) But, through prayer we:

- Enforce Satan's defeat in the heavenly realms so that God's kingdom may come to the earth.

- Enforce Satan's defeat in the earth so that people are enlightened to God's ways and are enabled to do His will.

Chapter 7 – Developing A Quiet Devotional Time with The Lord

Prayer as combat is to be the lifestyle of every believer. It is a means by which we become the light of the world and the salt of the earth. For we who are in Christ have been given authority over all evil spirits (see Luke 10:10 and Mark 16:17) and the spiritual weapons by which to demolish Satan's strongholds from the lives of those for whom we pray. (See 2 Corinthians 10:3-5.) Only as we engage in combat prayer can we effectively cooperate with God in seeing His kingdom purposes established.

SPIRITUAL WARFARE

The bible reveals that there is a war that started in heaven before the creation of humanity. It was a war of light against darkness, right against wrong, good against evil and life against death. The dragon, who lost in that battle in heaven, was hurled down and still exists. So, the battle is still raging down here, and we are right in the center of it.

Revelation 12:7 "And there was war in heaven......"

Today, it is a spiritual battle that we are in and we must fight it in the spirit.

2 Corinthians 10:3-4 "For though we live in the world, we do not wage war as the world does. The weapons we fight with are not weapons of the world. On the contrary they have divine power to demolish strongholds"

Our weapons of war are also spiritual weapons just as even the enemy is not physical, but spiritual.

Ephesians 6:10-18 "Finally my Brethren, be strong in the Lord and the power of His Might. Put on the whole armor of God that you may be able to stand against the wiles of the Devil. For we wrestle not against the flesh and blood but against principalities, against powers, against the rulers of the darkness of this world, against spiritual wickedness in high places. Wherefore take unto you

Chapter 7 – Developing A Quiet Devotional Time with The Lord

the whole armor of God that you may be able to withstand in the evil day and having done all to stand. Stand therefore, having your loins girt about with Truth and having on the breastplate of Righteousness and your feet shod with the Gospel of Peace. Above all, taking the shield of Faith wherewith you shall be able to quench all the fiery darts of the wicked. And take the Helmet of Salvation and the Sword of the Spirit, which is the Word of God. Praying always with all prayer and supplication in the Spirit and watching thereunto with all perseverance and supplication for all saints.

Matthew 11:12 "From the days of John the Baptist until now, the kingdom of God has suffered violence, and violent men take it by force.

CHAPTER 8 – COVENANT POSITIONING FOR EFFECTIVE PRAYER

The God of Abraham that we serve is a God of covenant. Throughout the history of humanity, He has worked with man on a covenant basis. This is mainly because man in fallen nature changes. This makes it difficult to have a consistent relationship with a covenant keeping God who does not change. So, God chose to set terms by which he will work with man. These terms are covenant terms and they come along with covenant terms and conditions, He makes a covenant with us. This automatically sets us into a covenant position. It is in this covenant position that we experience the abundant blessings of the Lord, the fulfillment of God's promises; protection, provision, healing, and the experience of answered prayers.

Examples of Covenant Terms and Conditions

Adam

Genesis 2:15-17 "The LORD God took the man and put him in the Garden of Eden to work it and take care of it. And the LORD God commanded the man, "You are free to eat from any tree in the garden; but you must not eat from the tree of the knowledge of

Chapter 8 – Covenant Positioning for Effective Prayer

good and evil, for when you eat from it you will certainly die."

Abraham

Genesis 17:3-7 "Abram fell facedown, and God said to him, as for me, this is my covenant with you: You will be the father of many nations. No longer will you be called Abram; your name will be Abraham, for I have made you a father of many nations. I will make you very fruitful; I will make nations of you, and kings will come from you. I will establish my covenant as an everlasting covenant between me and you and your descendants after you for the generations to come, to be your God and the God of your descendants after you.

Genesis 17:9-14 "Then God said to Abraham, as for you, you must keep my covenant, you and your descendants after you for the generations to come. This is my covenant with you and your descendants after you, the covenant you are to keep: Every male among you shall be circumcised. You are to undergo circumcision, and it will be the sign of the covenant between me and you. For the generations to come every male among you who is eight days old must be circumcised, including those born in your household or bought with money from a foreigner—those who are not your offspring. Whether born in your household or bought with your money, they must be circumcised. My covenant in your flesh is to be an everlasting covenant. Any uncircumcised male, who has not been circumcised in the flesh, will be cut off from his people; he has broken my covenant."

These and many others had distinctive covenants with their terms and conditions to be observed. God made the most superior covenant with the church. It was sealed by the blood of His son Jesus Christ. Whenever the church stands in the covenant position, all God's promises are fulfilled. There lies the secret of effective prayers.

Chapter 8 – Covenant Positioning for Effective Prayer

APPENDIX – ALL THE PRAYERS OF THE BIBLE

Prayer in the Old Testament

Genesis

Prayer History Begins	Gen. 4:26
Prayer and Spiritual Progress	Gen. 5:21-24
Prayer and the Altar	Gen. 12, 13
Prayer for an Heir	Gen. 15
Prayer—the Language of a Cry	Gen. 16
Prayer and Revelation	Gen. 17
Prayer for a Wicked City	Gen. 18, 19
Prayer after a Lapse	Gen. 20
Prayer of Obedience	Gen. 22
Prayer for a Bride	Gen. 24
Prayer for a Barren Wife	Gen. 25:19-23
Prayer Changes Things	Gen. 26
Prayer As a Vow,	Gen. 28
Prayer about a Wronged Brother	Gen. 32
Prayer—The Motion of a Hidden Fire	Gen. 39-41; 45:5-8; 50:20, 24
Prayer for Blessing upon the Tribes	Gen. 48, 4

Exodus

Prayer Expressed As a Groan	Exod. 1, 2
Prayer As a Dialogue	Exod. 3, 4

A

Prayer As Complaint ....Exod. 5-7
Prayer in League with Omnipotence ....Exod. 8-10
Prayer As Praise ....Exod. 15
Prayer in Peril ....Exod. 17
Prayer of the Needy...................................Exod. 22:22-24
Prayer for Delay of Deserved Judgment..............Exod. 32
First Prayer of Moses for Israel ....Exod. 32:9-14
Second Prayer of Moses ....Exod. 32:30-34
Third Prayer of Moses ....Exod. 33:12-23
Prayer and Transfiguration ....Exodus 34

Leviticus
None

Numbers
Prayer As Benediction ....Num. 6:24-27
Prayer for Preservation and Protection...Num. 10:35, 36
Prayer for the Removal of Judgment….........Num. 11:1, 2
Prayer of a Discouraged Heart ....Num. 11:10-35
Prayer of a Meek Man ....Num. 12
Prayer for the Upholding of Divine Honor..........Num. 14
Prayer for Divine Action against Rebellion..........Num. 16
Prayer for Relief from Death ....Num. 21
Prayer and Prophecy ....Num. 23, 24
Prayer for a New Leader ....Num. 27

Deuteronomy
Prayer for a Privileged Task ....Deut. 3:23-29

Prayer to One Who Is Nigh ....Deut. 4:7

Prayer for the Stay of Judgment...........Deut. 9:20, 26-29

Prayer as a Blessing ....Deut. 21:6-9

Prayer as Thanksgiving ....Deut. 26

Prayer as a Song...Deut. 32,33

Joshua

Prayer as a Challenge ....Josh. 5:13-15

Prayer God Does Not Answer ....Josh. 7

Prayer Neglected with Dire Results ....Josh. 9:14

Prayer That Produced a Miracle ....Josh. 10

Judges

Prayer for Direction ....Judg. 1

Prayer in Time of War ....Judg. 4, 5

Prayer for Signs ....Judg. 6

Prayer in Calamity ....Judg. 10:10-16

Prayer As a Bargain ....Judg. 11:30-40

Prayer for an Unborn Child ....Judg. 13

Prayer in the Face of Death ....Judg. 16:28-31

Prayer Directly Answered ....Judg. 20:23-28

Prayer for a Lost Tribe ....Judg. 21:2-3

Ruth

Benedictions

I Samuel

Prayer without Words ....I Sam. 1

Prayer, Prophetic in Outlook ....I Sam. 2:1-10

Prayer in the Sanctuary ....I Sam. 3

Prayer for National Trouble ....I Sam. 7

Prayer for a King...I Sam. 8

Prayer As Vindication ....I Sam. 12

Prayer of a Distressed King....................................I Sam. 14

Prayer of a Grieved Heart...................................I Sam. 15:11

Prayer As a Still Small Voice ....I Sam. 16:1-12

Prayer As the Secret of Courage ....I Sam. 17

Prayer As Enquiry ....I Sam. 23

Prayer for Deaf Ears ....I Sam. 28:7

Prayer for Restoration of War-Spoil ....I Sam. 30

II Samuel

Prayer As to Possession......................................II Sam. 2:1

Prayer for Victory Signs..............................II Sam. 5:19-25

Prayer for Blessing upon House and Kingdom…….. II Sam. 7:18-29

Prayer for a Sick Child ....II Sam. 12

Prayer As Pretense ....II Sam. 5:7-9

Prayer for Understanding of Affliction....II Sam. 21:1-12

Prayer As a Psalm ....II Sam. 22

Prayer As a Confession of Pride .... II Sam. 24:10-17

I Kings

Prayer for a Wise Heart ....I Kings 3

Prayer of Dedication ....I Kings 8:12-61

Prayer for a Withered Hand ....I Kings 13:6

D

Prayer for Closed Skies ....I Kings 17
Prayer for Resurrection of Dead Son ......I Kings 17:20-24
Prayer for Divine Honor ....I Kings 18:16-41
Prayer and Perseverance ....I Kings 18:45
Prayer for Death ....I Kings 19

II Kings
Prayer for a Dead Child............................II Kings 4:32-37
Prayer for Vision ....II Kings 6:13-17
Prayer for Deliverance from Defiant Foes ....II Kings 19
Prayer for Longer Life ....II Kings 20:1-11

I Chronicles
Prayer for Spiritual Prosperity ....I Chron. 4:9, 10
Prayer As Trust ....I Chron. 5:20
Prayer of Fear...I Chron. 13:12
Prayer for Establishment of Covenant ....I Chron. 17:16-27
Prayer Answered by Fire .... I Chron. 21
Prayer as a Sentinel .... I Chron. 23:30
Prayer and Giving ....I Chron. 29:10-19

II Chronicles
Prayer in National Danger ....II Chron. 14:11
Prayer and Reform ....II Chron. 15
Prayer and Appeal to History ....II Chron. 20:3-13
Prayer of Penitence ....II Chron. 33:13

Ezra

Prayer of Thanksgiving ....Ezra 7:27, 28
Prayer and Fasting ....Ezra 8:21-23
Prayer and Confession ....Ezra 9:5-10:4

Nehemiah

Prayer Born of Distress .... Neh. 1:4-11
Prayer in a Tight Corner ....Neh. 2:4
Prayer for Deliverance from Reproach ....Neh. 4:1-6
Prayer Triumphing Over Anger ....Neh. 4:7-9
Prayer and Restitution ....Neh. 5
Prayer against Craft ....Neh. 6:9-14
Prayer and the Word ....Neh. 8:1-13
Prayer and God's Goodness ....Neh. 9
Prayer for Remembrance........................Neh. 13:14, 22, 29, 31

Esther

The Watchful Care of God

Job

Prayer of Resignation ....Job 1:20-22
Prayer for Pity..Job 6:8, 9; 7:17-21
Prayer for Justification ....Job 9
Prayer, Job's Against Injustice ....Job 10
Prayer for Light on Immortality ....Job 14:13-22
Prayer and Profit ....Job 21:14-34
Prayer and Reason ....Job 23
Prayer Answered by Whirlwind ....Job 38

Prayer As Confession ....Job 40:3-5; 42:1-6
Prayei As Intercession ....Job 42:7-10

The Psalms

Prayer Born of Rebellion ....Ps. 3
Prayer of Holiness..Ps. 4
Prayer As a Morning Watch ....Ps. 5
Prayer for Divine Action...Ps. 7
Prayer of Praise for Divine Action ....Ps. 8
Prayer for Preservation Here and Hereafter ....Ps. 16
Prayer of the Cross ....Ps. 22
Prayer for Shepherd Care..Ps. 23
Prayer for the Manifestation of Divine Glory ....Ps. 24
Prayer as Ascent to God ....Ps. 25
Prayer of a Believing Heart...Ps. 27
Prayer As a Cameo of Christ ....Ps. 31
Prayer of a Tragic Soul..Ps. 32
Prayer for Protection against Enemies .... Ps. 35
Prayer in Praise of Loving-kindness................................. Ps. 36
Prayer of a Pilgrim .... Ps. 39
Prayer and Its Accomplishment .... Ps. 40
Prayer in Deep Distress .... Ps. 41
Prayer As a Door of Hope .... Ps. 42, 43
Prayer for Divine Assistance .... Ps. 44
Prayer for a Refuge .... Ps. 46
Prayer of a Broken Heart .... Ps. 51
Prayer at All Times .... Ps. 55

Prayer of Distress .... Ps. 57
Prayer of Trust .... Ps. 71
Prayer for God Himself.. Ps. 73
Prayer of a Pilgrim .... Pss. 90, 91
Prayer As Praise for God's Greatness............................. Ps. 96
Prayer for Escape from Trials .... Pss. 102, 103, 105
Prayer of Remembrance .... Ps. 106
Prayer for Those in Perils on Sea .... Ps. 107
Prayer and Affinity to Scripture .... Pss. 19, 119
Prayer for Searching of Heart .... Ps. 139

Proverbs
Prayers as the Channel of Wisdom

Ecclesiastes
Prayer and Fatalism

Song of Solomon
Prayer's Secret

Isaiah
Prayer God Does Not Hear ....Isa. 1:15; 16:12
Prayer and Cleansing.. Isa. 6
Prayer for a Sign... Isa. 7:11
Prayer of Exaltation... Isa. 12
Prayer of Praise for Triumphs.. Isa. 25
Prayer for Peace .... Isa. 26
Prayer and Confidence .... Isa. 41

Prayer and Practice .... Isa. 55
Prayer Unpopular to Many... Isa. 59
Prayer — Watcher .... Isa. 62
Prayer for Display of Divine Power.......................... Isa. 63, 64

Jeremiah
Prayer As Confession of Inability .... Jer. 1
Prayer As Mourning for Backsliding .... Jer. 2, 3
Prayer As Complaint .... Jer. 4:10-31
Prayer of Lament over Rebellion....................................... Jer. 5
Prayer from a Prison .... Jer. 6
Prayer Forbidden .... Jer. 7:16
Prayer for Justice .... Jer. 10:23-25
Prayer of Perplexity .... Jer. 12:1-4
Prayer for Relief from Sin and Drought .... Jer. 14:7-22
Prayer for Divine Vengeance .... Jer. 15:15-21
Prayer for Confusion of Enemies......... Jer. 16:19-21, 17:13-18
Prayer for Overthrow of Evil Counsel .... Jer. 18:18-23
Prayer of a Despairing Heart .... Jer. 20:7-13
Prayer of Gratitude for Divine Goodness .... Jer. 32:16-25
Prayer for a Believing Remnant .... Jer. 42

Lamentations
Prayer of Pain ....Lam. 1:20-22
Prayer for Pity ....Lam. 2:19-22
Prayer As Complaint .... Lam. 3.147
Prayer for the Oppressed .... Lam. 5

Eekiel

Prayer As Protest .... Ezek. 4:14

Prayer for Preservation of Residue .... Ezek. 9:8-11

Prayer Sanctuary... Ezek. 11:13-16

Daniel

Prayer for Interpretation.. Dan. 2:17, 18

Prayer in Defiance of Decree .... Dan. 6:10-15

Prayer of Confession .... Dan. 9

Prayer and Its Spiritual Results .... Dan. 10

Prayer for Light on One's End............................. Dan. 12:8-13

Hosea

Prayer —Its Many Sidelights

Joel

Prayer in Emergency .... Joel 1:19, 20

Prayer and Weeping .... Joel 2:17

Amos

Prayer for Respite and Forgiveness, ... Amos 7:1-9

Obadiah

Prayer Absent in This Brief Book

Jonah

Prayer of Heathen Sailors................................... Jonah 1:14-16

Prayer Out of Hell .... Jonah 2

Prayer of a Repentant City... Jonah 3

Prayer of a Displeased Prophet .... Jonah 4

Micah
Prayer Is Looking and Waiting

Nahum
Prayer Finds No Place in This Book of Judgment

Habakkuk
Prayer of Complaint and Vindication .... Hab. 1:1-4, 12-17
Prayer of Faith .... Hab. 3

Zephaniah
Prayers Absent but Implied

Haggai
Prayer Assumed, Not Mentioned

Zechariah
Prayer Aspects

Malachi
Prayer — Protest One .... Mal. 1:2
Prayer — Protest Two .... Mal. 1:6
Prayer — Protest Three.. Mal. 1:7, 13
Prayer — Protest Four... Mal. 2:17
Prayer — Protest Five... Mal. 3:17
Prayer - Protest Six .... Mal. 3:8

Prayers and Prayer in the New Testament

Prayer As Practiced by Christ

Prayer at His baptism	Luke 3: 21-22
Prayer after a crowded day	Luke 4:42; Mark 1:35
Prayer as an escape from popularity	Luke 5:15-16
Prayer after a trying day	Mark 6:30-31
Prayer with His own	Luke 9:18-31
Prayer on the mount	Luke 9:29
Prayer ater success	Luke 10:21
Prayer as a habit	Luke 11:1
Prayer at a grave	John 11:41-42
Prayer on a mountain	Mark 6:46
Prayer of anguish	John 12:27-28
Prayer for a backsliding disciple	Luke 22:31-32
Prayer of the Great High Priest	John Ch. 17
Prayer in Gethsemane	Lu 22:39-46; Matt 26:36-46: Jo 18:1
Prayer from the cross	Luke 23:34-46

Matthew

Prayer and the Necessity of Forgiveness	Matt. 5:22-26; 6:12, 14, 15
Prayer and Hypocrisy	Matt. 6:5-7; Luke 11:1-4
Prayer As Taught by Christ	Matt. 6:8-13
Prayer As Specified by Christ	Matt. 7:7-11
Prayer of a Leper	Matt. 8:1-4

Prayer of the Centurion .... Matt. 8:5-13
Prayer in Peril .... Matt. 8:23-27
Prayer of Maniacs .... Matt. 8:28-34
Prayer of Jairus .... Matt. 9:18, 19
Prayer of the Diseased Woman .... Matt. 9:20-22
Prayer of Two Blind Men .... Matt. 9:27-31
Prayer for Laborers .... Matt. 9:37-39
Prayer of Christ's Gratitude to God .... Matt. 11:25-27
Prayer on a Mountain .... Matt. 14:23
Prayer of Peter in Distress .... Matt. 14:28-30
Prayer of Syro-Phoenician Woman .... Matt. 15:21-28
Prayer for a Lunatic Son .... Matt. 17:14-21
Prayer in Unity .... Matt. 18:19, 20
Prayer in a Parable .... Matt. 18:23-35
Prayer for a Privileged Position .... Matt. 20:20-28
Prayer for Healing of Blindness .... Matt. 20:29-34
Prayer of Faith .... Matt. 21:18-22
Prayer of Pretense .... Matt. 23: 14, 25
Prayer of Accountability .... Matt. 25:20, 22, 24
Prayer of a Resigned Will .... Matt. 26:26, 36-46
Prayer at Calvary .... Matt. 27:46, 50

Mark

Prayer of a Demon .... Mark 1:23-28, 32-34
Prayer — Habits of Christ .... Mark 1:35; 6:4
Prayer for the Deaf and Dumb .... Mark 7:31-37
Prayer and Fasting .... Mark 2:18; 9:29

Prayer of the Young Ruler .... Mark 10:17-22

Luke Prayer of Zacharias............................ Luke 1:8, 13; 67-80

Prayer As a Magnificat .... Luke 1:46-55

Prayer As Adoration.................................. Luke 2:10-20; 25-38

Prayer at the Portal of Service .... Luke 3:21, 22

Prayer As Escape from Popularity .... Luke 5:16

Prayer and the Twelve .... Luke 6:12, 13, 20, 28

Prayer and Transfiguration .... Luke 9:28, 29

Prayer in Parable Form.. Luke 11:5-13

Prayer of the Prodigal............................ Luke 15:11-24, 29, 30

Prayer out of Hell... Luke 16:22-31

Prayer of Ten Lepers .... Luke 17:12-19

Prayer in Parable Form.. Luke 18:1-8

Prayer of Pharisee and Publican............................ Luke 18:9-14

Prayer for Peter's Preservation .... Luke 22:31, 32

Prayer of Agony.. Luke 22:39-46

Prayer and the Risen Lord .... Luke 24:30, 50-53

John

Prayer for the Spirit........... John 4:9, 15, 19, 28; 7:37-39; 14:16

Prayer of a Nobleman.. John 4:46-54

Prayer for the Bread of Life .... John 6:34

Prayer for Confirmation .... John 11:40-42

Prayer with a Double Aspect.............................. John 12:27, 28

Prayer As a Privilege .... John 14:13-15; 15:16; 16:23-26

Prayer of All Prayers.. John 17.226

Acts

Prayer in the Upper Chamber .... Acts 1:13, 14
Prayer for a Successor.. Acts 1:15-26
Prayer and Worship .... Acts 2:42-47
Prayer As an Observance .... Acts 3:1
Prayer for Boldness of Witness .... Acts 4:23-31
Prayer and the Ministry of the Word .... Acts 6:4-7
Prayer of the First Martyr .... Acts 7:55-60
Prayer for Samaritans and a Sorcerer .... Acts 8:9-25
Prayer of a Convert .... Acts 9:5, 6, 11
Prayer for Dorcas, ... Acts 9:36-43
Prayer of Cornelius.. Acts 10:2-4,9, 31
Prayer for Peter in Prison .... Acts 12:5, 12-17
Prayer of Ordination .... Acts 13:2, 3, 43
Prayer with Fasting....................... Acts 13:2, 3; 14:15, 23, 26
Prayer at the Riverside.. Acts 16:13, 16
Prayer in a Dungeon .... Acts 16:25, 34
Prayer of Committal... Acts 20:36
Prayer in a Shipwreck... Acts 27:33, 35
Prayer for the Fever-Stricken .... Acts 28:8, 15, 28

Romans

Prayer for a Prosperous Journey .... Rom. 1:8-15
Prayer Inspired by the Spirit .... Rom. 8:15, 23, 26, 27
Prayer for Israel's Sake................................... Rom. 10:1; 11:26
Prayer As a Continuing .... Ministry; Rom. 12:12
Prayer for Like-Mindedness...................... Rom. 15:5,6, 30-33

Prayer for Satan's Conquest .... Rom. 16:20, 24-27

I Corinthians
Several Facets of Prayer Mentioned

II Corinthians
Prayer as a Benediction .... II Cor. 1:2-4
Prayer for Removal of Thorn, ... II Cor. 12:7-10

Galatians
Prayer-facets, But No Prayers

Ephesians
Prayer and the Believer's Position .... Eph. 1:1-11
Prayer for Perception and Power .... Eph. 1:15-20
Prayer As Access to God .... Eph. 2:18; 3:12
Prayer for Inner Fullness .... Eph. 3:13-21
Prayer and Inner Melody .... Eph. 5:19, 20
Prayer As a Warrior's Reserve .... Eph. 6:18, 19

Philippians
Prayer As a Request for Joy .... Phil. 1:2-7
Prayer and Peace of Mind .... Phil. 4:6, 7, 19-23

Colossians
Prayer As Praise for Loyalty .... Col. 1:1-8
Prayer for a Seven-fold Blessing .... Col. 1:9-14
Prayer Fellowship .... Col. 4:2-4, 12, 17

I Thessalonians
Prayer of Remembrance .... I Thess. 1:1-3
Prayer for a Return Visit .... I Thess. 3:9-13
Prayer, Praise and Perfection .... I Thess. 5:17, 18, 23, 24, 28

II Thessalonians
Prayer for Worthiness of Calling............... II Thess. 1:3, 11, 12
Prayer for Comfort and Stability............. II Thess. 2:13, 16, 17
Prayer for the Word and Protection .... II Thess. 3:1-5. .257

I Timothy
A Few Pertinent References to Prayer

II Timothy
Prayer for Timothy's Ministry, ... II Tim. 1:2-7
Prayer for the House of Onesiphorus....................................... II Tim. 1:6-18
Prayer for False Friends .... II Tim. 4:14-18

Titus
Prayerless, Apart from Salutation at Benediction

Philemon

Glimpses of the Range of Prayer's Effectiveness

Hebrews
Prayer As Praise for Creation .... Heb. 1:10-12
Prayer for Mercy and Favor...Heb. 4:16
Prayer and Ministry of Christ .... Heb. 5:7, 8; 7:24, 25
Prayer for the Outworking of God's Will.......Heb. 12:9, 12, 15

Prayer for Perfectness .... Heb. 13:20, 21

James
Prayer for Wisdom .... Jas. 1:5-8, 17
Prayer That Misses the Target................................... Jas. 4:2, 3
Prayer That Prevails .... Jas. 5:13-18

I Peter
Prayer of Gratitude for Inheritance......................... I Pet. 1:3, 4
Prayer in the Married State ....I Pet. 3:7-12
Prayer-Watch... I Pet. 4:7
Prayer for Christian Stability .... I Pet. 5:10, 11

II Peter
Prayer for Multiplication of Grace and Peace .... II Peter 1:2

I John
Prayer Is Everywhere Implied

II John
Prayer Not Mentioned .... Apart from Verse 3

III John
Prayer the Background of Reputation .... III John 1-4,12

Jude
Prayer in the Spirit .... Jude 20

Revelation
Prayer As Praise to the Lamb for Redemption .... Rev. 5:9

Prayer As Golden Incense .... Rev. 5:8, 8:3
Prayer of the Martyred Host .... Rev. 6:10
Prayer of the Gentile Host .... Rev. 7:9-12
Prayer of the Elders .... Rev. 11:15-19
Prayer of Moses .... Rev. 15:3, 4
Prayer of the Glorified Saints.............................. Rev. 19:1-10
Prayers Ending the Bible................................... Rev. 22:17, 20